MORE PRAISE FOR *Santiago Sketches*

"Santiago Sketches *is a gift box brimming with luminous local details of a loved place through which—over a space of nine months—the poet moves like a pilgrim of the senses, offering in poem after poem what's been seen, felt, smelled, heard; what's been touched, tasted, and understood: "Flap of a pigeon's wing. / A dark-eyed girl in purple slippers..." "an angel raises a star / among the horses…" "At the fountain, the junkies / washing their needles." What McLoghlin has composed in this adventurous new collection is a scrupulously tolerant anatomy of Santiago, a religious, secular, open-eyed, warts-and-all love letter to a city where he—a stranger—managed for a little, unforgettable while to make himself at home."*

EAMON GRENNAN
Guggenheim Fellow and author of ten poetry collections

MORE PRAISE FOR DAVID MCLOGHLIN

"As an avid reader of Irish literature, I found David McLoghlin's work… to be fresh and unexpected, yet still worthy of inclusion in the great canon of poetry that is produced by his nation."

"Its own heroic achievement."

BILLY COLLIN

"These are big, ambitious, sometimes sprawling poems, rich in narrative and in detail."

MOYA CANNON & THEO DORGAN
Judges' Citation, The Patrick Kavanagh Awards, 2008

"David McLoghlin's debut collection Waiting for Saint Brendan and Other Poems *proves strong on first reading and grows richer… with each subsequent rereading. …The poems are rhetorically baroque, inward-looking and taut with imagery, and his complex metaphors unfold, slow and origami-like, often across multiple stanzas. …This is a necessary book, one well worth reading and returning to."*

ERIC BLIMAN, *Birmingham Poetry Review*

Santiago Sketches
David McLoghlin

salmonpoetry
*Publishing Irish & International
Poetry Since 1981*

Published in 2017 by
Salmon Poetry
Cliffs of Moher, County Clare, Ireland
Website: www.salmonpoetry.com
Email: info@salmonpoetry.com

ISBN 978-1-910669-75-4

COVER IMAGE: "*Rúa das Hortas, Santiago de Compostela*",
Watercolour, 31 x 23 cm, by Val McLoughlin. www.valmcloughlin.com

COVER DESIGN & TYPESETTING: *Siobhán Hutson*

Printed in Ireland by Sprint Print

Salmon Poetry gratefully acknowledges the support of
The Arts Council / An Chomhairle Ealaoín

For my wife, Adrienne

Acknowledgements

Grateful acknowledgement is due to the editors of the following publications, where some of these poems first appeared, sometimes in a slightly different form:

Éire-Ireland: An Interdisciplinary Journal of Irish Studies ("A Selection of New Irish Poets", edited by Kelly Sullivan, vol. 48, issues 3&4, autumn / winter 2013); *Dream of a City: An Anthology of Contemporary Poetry from Limerick City of Culture* (Astrolabe Press, 2014); *The Stony Thursday Book* (issue 13, autumn 2014); *Cyphers* (issue 80, 2015); *The Limerick Post*, 11th March, 2015; *Estudios Irlandeses* (online, issue 12, 2017).

I would like to thank the Instituto da lingua galega (ILGA) for grants that allowed me to return to Santiago de Compostela in the summers of 2003, 2004 and 2005 to study Galician (*galego*). Grateful thanks to Eiléan Ní Chuilleanáin, Kimiko Hahn, Eamon Grennan and John Liddy, and to Germán Asensio for translating many of these poems into Spanish for *Estudios Irlandeses*. Thank you to Adrienne Brock, Thomas Dooley, Peter Longofono and Patrick Loughnane for reading the manuscript, and to Cristián Gómez-Olivares. Thank you to Dr. Philip Johnston of University College, Dublin, and to my Erasmus shipmates: Andy Ellis, Olga Nuñez, John Lynch, Mark Sabine, Tony Shiplee, Julian Loftus, Spencer Willbanks and Matt Stevens, Angela Cañellas, Sarah Rollinson, Vanessa McCormack, Geraldine and Laetitia, Thomas and Nacho, Francis Bandín Potel and Manuel, Xesús (Suso) Vázquez, and Fátima Cobo. Thank you to the Pombo family, especially Regina, with fond memories of Fernando. And to many friends in Galicia over the years for their generosity and hospitality. Truly, as someone was once heard to say at a café terrace in the Rías Altas one summer evening, "esto es vida, José. Esto es vida."

Thank you to Jessie Lendennie and Siobhán Hutson at Salmon Poetry, and to my parents, whose support allowed me to go to Santiago in the first place.

I am the place in which something has happened.

—Claude Lévi-Strauss

Bird of Time—
in Kyoto pining
for Kyoto.

—Matsuo Bashō
(Tr. by Lucien Stryk)

But there never was any city but the one.
—Samuel Beckett, "The Calmative"
in *Stories and Texts for Nothing*

INTRODUCTION

Details Into Light [1]

by JOHN LIDDY

It has been said of David McLoghlin's first collection, *Waiting for Saint Brendan* (Salmon Poetry, 2012), that "These are big, ambitious, sometimes sprawling poems, rich in narrative and in detail, an autobiography of sorts, where the voyaging soul is concerned to find home and meaning in a dialogue between self and other." (Moya Cannon and Theo Dorgan, The Patrick Kavanagh Awards, Judges' Citation, 2008.) It has also been noted, by poet Ed Skoog, that McLoghlin "unites sharp 'eye work', in rich and telling detail, with what Rilke called 'heart work', in a series of clear and powerful images." I found the book to be the work of a courageous poet, particularly in section two, where he confronts his own demons as Brendan confronted his.

With regard to this book, for "sketches" we could read "details" because the poems are made from observations in little notebooks kept during a year in Santiago de Compostela and then transferred to bigger page-a-day diaries that the poet bought in those "great Spanish stationery shops." (In conversation with David McLoghlin.)

I remember watching the poet Desmond O'Grady jot down words on torn corners of newspaper pages and carefully fold the tiny pieces of writing and place them in his wallet. Also, I once came across a poem by Heaney on display in the British Library, written on the inside of a Kellogg's Cornflakes box. We all have our methods and anything will do, really: beer mats, paper serviettes, cigarette boxes, even mobile phones; they all serve the poem, helping it along towards the printed page or to never see the light of day again. Thankfully, we have McLoghlin's perseverance and "eye work" that has given us, in these poems, an outsider's / insider's view of the ordinary, day-to-day happenings in Santiago.

These are not "big, ambitious, sometimes sprawling poems" but rather ethereal, worked-on but not overworked, slightly-controlled reactions to what caught his eye. Instead of photographs, we have photowords. Glimpses, gleanings, scratches and scrapings of life as he experienced it during the course of a year in that great pilgrim City of Galicia. They are the poet's own searchings on a voyage that would eventually take him to New York.

In a sense, these poems are a pilgrim's store of experiences and longings brought to us by a keen-eyed poet: from 'Café Derby' we read of the waiter who could have served Valle Inclán (how we wish for those *tertulias* again), the bikers in the Obradoiro, and the zinc bar counter (not many left now). In 'Lamed' we are treated to a wonderful juxtaposition of proud, Napoleonic-type strollers and the medieval clerk wearing a four-inch-orthopedic shoe; elsewhere, the presence of the Moors—never too far from us in Spain. 'Map' makes the connection with Ireland and West Clare cheekbones, and 'Civil Disagreement' is a snapshot of Spain's old political divide. We are back with McLoghlin's penchant for saints in 'All Saints' and the day, 1st November, tastes of the saint's bones (a type of bun); the sound as old fingers rake the dominos (an exact image) and the poet's imaginary escape from the spewing rain to the smells of late summer in Nerja, a thousand kilometres to the south, where the younger McLoghlin used to holiday with his parents.

From here we enter the terrain of people and place and the details that go into making up their lives. In 'Pepe's Wife' we can see into her "sad apron eyes"; the traditional pipers and their flaccid bagpipes like deserters from "a forgotten peninsular war"; the gong of the poet's silence and the call to prayer (McLoghlin cannot avoid it!); a walk past unofficial shebeen bars, and the glassed-in balconies are sun traps (they also provide winter warmth). We are back in familiar territory with the seven-year wait for a holy door to open as the poet pokes fun at the 12 apostles, while someone else has painted their lips with lipstick. Rain again, as Beckett said, while the priest ignores the beggar and life is a lottery ticket, a street sweeper, a junkie, the poet's dead grandfather in a suburban fir tree in Dublin via Santiago, and the overgrown moss on the cathedral is a beard. Víctor Jara's broken hands are recalled in 'Antonio', a poem about a busker, second chances, Basque rebels and the poet's refusal to play the Irish card. In 'Evening, Quintana' we have the café life of dark-haired men, and in the companion pieces, a medieval pilgrim from Dingle (one of the *caminos*, and the place where the poet lived for a few years) writ in stone; and gypsies jamming.

'The Book of Beginnings', 'First Night' and 'Leaving'— each poem is a return to the time when his Santiago experience began. They speak naturally, from hindsight, of sharing cigarettes with old female acquaintances; that Iberian confidence and penchant for profanity that would be shocking in more prudish societies; an epiphany in his old *barrio*, and that predawn walk of loneliness and discovery.

These sketches or searchings are better than any tourist guide. The information is precise, accurate and loyal to people and place. With a little imagination, the reader will relish the detail and if the urge is carried to its conclusion, you could do worse than go to Santiago with these poems in your pocket to guide you. They are the stuff of a poet's pilgrimage, homages to a place that helped him to grow and to complete some of that dialogue with himself and the other. Is not this what the *camino* is all about.

[1] First published in *Estudios Irlandeses* (issue 12, March 2017) www.estudiosirlandeses.org/2017/03/. John Liddy has published several books of poetry, some with translations in Spanish, and books of stories for children. His latest book is *The Secret Heart of Things* (Revival Press, Limerick, 2014). Another book is forthcoming. He is the founding editor, along with Jim Burke, of *The Stony Thursday Book* literary journal.

Author's Note

These poems were written between October 1993 and June 1994, on a year abroad in Santiago de Compostela. Santiago is the capital of Galicia, that region in northwestern Spain which, on the map, looks as if it might rather be part of Portugal. The first I heard of Santiago was in second year at University College, Dublin, when Dr. Philip Johnston, the lecturer in 20th century Spanish poetry and the Erasmus coordinator, interrupted his class on the Generation of '27 to say: "Now, remember: this year, we're partnering with Madrid, Bilbao, Valencia, Valladolid, Murcia, Lugo and Santiago de Compostela. Places will fill up fast, so sign up well before the deadline, if you're interested."

It was the Hilary term, maybe late January. My twenty-year-old, long-haired self was busy slipping late essays under professors' doors, and entirely skipped Old and Middle English tutorials to spend most days in the bowels of the Arts block, rehearsing Dramsoc plays and partying after performances in the Montrose Hotel. But somehow I managed to fill out the application on time. Several weeks later, Dr. Johnston called me in to meet with him. His office was at the end of the corridor, near the pigeon holes, and dangerously close to Professor Gallagher's door, the head of department whose class on Góngora I was barely passing.

I'd put Santiago first on the list. (I don't remember my second choice.) I'd been to Madrid and didn't want to go to a capital city. I knew the lesser-spoilt nooks of the Costa del Sol and—foolishly—imagined the Costa Blanca to be much the same, or worse, so Murcia didn't interest me. I didn't feel drawn by Valladolid. And if I went to Valencia, I'd have to fight against a local dialect of Catalan to improve my Spanish.[2] In Bilbao, ETA was still active, and Spaniards

---

[2] I didn't realise Galicia was bilingual too, or know about Valencia's orange-blossom-soaked location on the Mediterranean, or Las Fallas: the carnival where all the gloriously-satirical papier-mâché sculptures and floats are burnt on the last night.

dismissed the city as a valley of factories, with a river black from industrial waste.[3] And in 1993, Lugo was a backwater (it has improved greatly since). Santiago was the enigma. Apart from a rumour about a pilgrimage, all I knew was that our Spanish family friend, Fernando Pombo, called it the "Ireland of Spain", and that the Galicians were famous emigrators.

Dr. Johnston said: "David, I'll give you Santiago, as long as I can be a hundred percent sure you won't back out on me." I was a dead cert, I told him, and promptly forgot about it.— Until the information packet arrived that summer at my parents' house, and I realised I was really going.

*

At *Aduanas*, the agent opened my passport, checking my photo against my face. I noticed the insignia on his pillbox hat, the axe across a bundle of sticks, the *fasces*, and started getting nervous. I was always nervous when the Guardia Civil were on the scene. They had taken Franco's side in the Civil War, and their motto was still *Todo Por La Patria*, "Everything For The Fatherland". They were and still are a paramilitary police force, and older Spaniards either hated them or respected them, and even those that respected them had an edge of fear in their respect.

He raised his eyes again, then palmed my passport firmly, almost hard, onto the Formica counter.

"Bienvenido," he said, without smiling.

Arrivals smelled of black, filterless tobacco and strong, almost sweet, aftershave. Mine was the only arriving flight: Iberia from Dublin via Heathrow. Groups of police hung around, idle and watchful, their thumbs hooked in their ammunition belts. Between suitcases, the baggage handlers unselfconsciously adjusted their crotches, their blue jumpsuits open almost to the waist, like stevedores. The only

---

[3] Pre-Guggenheim, the world was yet to discover the glories of the *pintxo*, and Basque cuisine—or, indeed, the glories of the Basque Country in general.

female presences were the tired middle-aged cleaners who contrasted with the women in Foreign Exchange with highlighted blonde hair and perfect make up.

The pair of Guardia Civil at the exit were wearing patent-leather tricorn hats that made them like weird minotaurs, and that told me: *you're in Spain, now*.

But a smell of wet grass was coming through the finger of window the taxi driver had left open, and there was a chill in the air. On the Malaga coast, even in early October there'd be cicadas, and a vestige of the heat smell, and jasmine. Here, we passed strange pyramidal hayricks, the tops of which were covered in tarpaulin, and houses were almost alpine. The landscape seemed Swiss, or Austrian: like the lowlands before the foothills of Alps that never came. Empty nightclubs flashed their purple neon signs in the rain.

After some unpromising suburbs, we came to the edge of the pedestrianised old city: a harmony of brown granite. All I saw was a square of palm trees harried by rain. The taxi drew up in a puddle and the driver turned to me: "Plaza de Galicia, joven."

*

The square was the nineteenth-century breakwater between the crass 1960s new town and the baroque Old Town's rain-softened stone, where moss was growing from naiads' mouths, features blurred as if they'd been underwater for centuries, the streets paved with the same stone as the houses; the buildings with balconies glassed over to form conservatories, white wood between old panes, and arcades under the apartments, where there were bookshops and cheese shops, shops advertising "Ultramarinos": *from across the sea*. Lichens grew from gutters, which were rusting, bleeding drops of rust blood onto the paving stones. The continuation of Praza de Galicia, between the Old Town and the new town's concrete, was the Alameda park, and along it was the street that seemed to end in Capela do Pilar, especially in the evening. The sun would set in wet orange streaks behind the chapel's bell tower and the silhouettes of palm trees where blackbirds clamoured in the evenings. Later I imagined the palm trees had been brought back as seeds from Cuba—after the defeat of 1898, when Spain lost its empire—brought back mixed in with diamonds, moveable wealth, to the place all the emigrants had started from: the Galicians who'd settled everywhere from Patagonia to Puerto Rico. "Hai un galego na lúa," they like to say about themselves. There's a Galician on the moon.[4]

I didn't know any of this. I didn't know it was a pilgrim city, that it was a thousand years old, one of the "Big Three", along with Rome and Jerusalem. I didn't know the story had begun before me. I found Hostal Maycar, and dropped my bag. I phoned my parents and my friend Regina Pombo in Madrid, but the *Telefónica* phone gobbled my pesetas before I could say much. I saw a café across the square with jockey paraphernalia on the awning that read *Café Derby*.

---

[4] In Argentina, Spaniards are nicknamed "gallegos". Spanish has no exact word for homesickness, and uses a Galician loan word, "morriña".

October

Café Derby, First Night

Past the leaky umbrella bin of dark wood,
girl facing boy, four teenagers play seriously
at adulthood. The boys' hair is bullfighter-gelled,
engominado. French-style, each girl wears a sweater,
pastel, around her shoulders, another at the waist.
They are attended by a small bald waiter
who might have apprenticed at the *tertulias*
of Valle Inclán. Hieratic, a slight limp,
the collarless white coat buttoned to the neck,
unhurrying, he carries a tray to their table—
the dark, thick hot chocolate from the Americas,
the infusions in alchemical jars, unfurling.

Roads start at *Kilómetro Cero*
in the Door of the Sun.
I've come to live at the other one.

                              (5th October)

Colexiata do Sar

Half past two in the afternoon: metal shutters
slamming down. Shade this side of the street.
A greased-back black-haired guy—smoker's cough—
goes by. Cars, then silence of a side-street
on Saturday afternoon. Flap of a pigeon's wing.
A dark-eyed girl in purple slippers with her boyfriend.
This suburb, almost countryside. In the shade of the Romanesque
church: wedding rice. A white terrier barking at me.

Two elderly women in buffalo fur coats
—like the campaign coats of centurions—
stand at the zinc counter
of the male-dominated bar, talking at
each other: small, gesticulating upwards.
Old men frown, slapping down dominoes.

Lamed

Among the proud walkers, each one his own Napoleon
—only briefly perturbed as a 6 foot 4 blond German
passes in rope sandals—go the ones hobble-walking
through the drizzle of medieval streets.
And apart from a briefcase and beige gabardine,
the small man with the four-inch black orthopedic
platform shoe could be medieval
—that sense of the afflicted.

Everyone going out in different directions
past the old men in black berets
on park benches
talking in increasing darkness.

(15th October)

In O'Curruncho with Mark and Emma

A bit like
when I was a child
when I watched people reading
—I caressed the insides
of my arms,
loving inwardness—
I'm watching
the rolling
of a cigarette
by the stranger
who has just asked Emma
for some tobacco
and stands there at the table
rolling it in silence.

A knight in exile, paying for his drinks
without a smile, but straight-backed, proud
and tired. With the group, though set apart—
tall, grey hair like an egret tuft,
he stands watching the card players.

(23rd October)

Portico of Glory

Ahead of me, under heaven's musicians
—a trad session in ecstasy—
Christ's lineage carved above us,
a pilgrim is fitting his fingers
into the impression
centuries of hands have made
on the Tree of Jesse. I slot my hand
into the invisible
hand—a faith negative.

Tir na nÓg

for Francis

"¿David, qué es 'Tear Na Nog-gay?'" you ask,
hesitant, mispronouncing the Irish—
"what's *Tír na nÓg?*"—and I start
to fall in love with you.

We were 20 when you asked me that.
They call it Rúa Nova because of the street it's on:
our corner table, veined white marble
on cast-iron legs, the café doesn't have a name.

Map

Sky up through the narrow streets.
Old men in berets and suits leaning on sticks
talking outside Casa das Crechas
where copper coins glint between the stones
around an Elizabethan map of Ireland.
Dark, bearded young men,
cheek wisps above the beard line.
Strong, *galego*-speaking women
with Al-Andalus eyes, smoking Ducados.
One of them turns: West Clare
in her cheekbones. Her hazel eyes, to me,
have the intensity of someone young
in an old photograph—taken in Quilty,
a summer day—through a long exposure.

Civil Disagreement

A punky young woman
muffled in a PLO scarf, dark-eyed,
all determined anarchism and the Basque mullet,
gets on the bus—an old, blue 1950s city bus—
and says to the driver in *galego*:
"Praza Roxa, por favor." Red Square.
A man with a black moustache
growls in Castilian:
"¡*Plaza* José Antonio Primo de Rivera!"

(30th October)

November

All Saints

Forearms in sugar dust, the baker relishes
saying, "¡hoxe comemos ósos de santo!"
We eat the saint's bones on All Saints day!
Biting down, I get to the sweet
marrow of it.

Old men's caps and coats hang on hooks.
A cheesy, low-cut variety show on Telecinco
on mute. Oblivious, stony-faced,
they rake the dominoes, rake through bones.
At the next table, a card player flicks one down
onto once-plush baize, and turns away
with the contempt of the defeated.

Pepe's Bar

The long empty bar in the afternoon.
Strong café con leche: brown stain of milk.
Smell of a cigarette just lit.
A gravel voice says: "oye, Pepe."
Pepe brings the drink to the back room.
He knows by the voice what to bring.

In Praza de Platerías
—square of the silver-beaters—
an angel raises a star
among the horses that are about
to jump
out of the fountain.

Santiago Matamoros

In the cathedral, with a mad gleam
Saint James the Moor-slayer sweeps off
forty-thousand heads.

Under the spout drains in the Old Town
—monsters' mouths spewing rain—
I'm thinking of Nerja
a thousand kilometres to the south.
In November the air in Andalusia
still holds a *deje* of summer
—Almonds, sea salt, faded jasmine.
Faint bruise—a trace.

Pepe's Wife

When you go to pay,
she never accepts the money,
motioning you to him with her eyes
—eyes of flies in close-up
crawling on *tapas*, eyes of hair, greasy
from frying *tortilla*,
fat, sad apron eyes.

Año Santo

It's November. Holy Year almost over.
They'll close the Puerta Santa
for six years.

Walking down a sunset street
all the smells of evening.
An old man with his wife
his fat, cropped, short-hair neck.
Faint moped fumes.
Familiar smell again.

Old women, bouffant hairstyles,
puffed up in black fur coats, talking, talking.
A colonial bell tower with sky through it;
palm trees in the north.
Black birds in the trees.
Groups of joggers through the park.
Deep burning streaks of sun
between dark hills.

The sound of water from fountains;
branches losing their leaves.
Thursday night.
Soon the students will be going out.
In the park, a boy and a girl walk their Alsatian.
Old men in berets, walking.
And me.

Near the cathedral, an open window to the night.
A scallop shell in sandstone above the door.
Blue fire from a workshop;
men in light-blue overalls. Half-past seven.

A woman whispers something as I pass.
Half-closed eyes, red eyelids, greasy long hair.
I go on. Police car pauses near the park.
Ratty fur coat, cheap heels.
She lurches on.

A car leaves the Reis Católicos' garage.
Doormen, glass doors.
Taxi—green light on top—passes.

A white-haired priest leaves by a side door
after Mass, walking into the night.
In a clothes shop
a woman lights a cigarette.
The Quintana is quiet.

November. The door still open.
The year about to close.

Seven years 'til I come back.

Antonio

Most nights, there was a busker in the arch under Bishop Xelmirez's palace—the acoustics so good, you heard him long before you came up the stairs from the Obradoiro. He sat because of the long hours, and when he stood he walked as if his leg was turned the wrong way around. I didn't know his name. Ten years later, at midnight Lucía and I were walking down from Cervantes, Santiago starting again for me. He was playing "Te Recuerdo, Amanda" by Víctor Jara. "¡Claro!" he said to her, "you played at singer-songwriter nights at Modus Vivendi!" His girlfriend came to collect him with their Golden Retriever. She was a student, 10 years younger than him. As they walked away, I thought of second chances, and Lucía's student days when she said "every window was open playing Pablo Milanés, Mercedes Sosa, and Silvio," Latin American hope songs. Behind the songs, *compañeros*, was Víctor Jara—and me and her missing each other in every Old Town bar, me missing being in a different book.

Tarasca sometimes played the hope songs, but more often rebel songs, flew the Basque Ikurrina beside the Cuban star. When I ordered in Spanish, the bearded bartender looked at me askance under black-and-white photos of prisoners, friends of the axe and the asp—echoes of a mural iconography. He turned stony, I wouldn't play the Irish card. Off my elbow, a local wore the balaclava and the armalite, foregrounded on the Tricolour: an easy t-shirt. Víctor Jara on the jukebox.

"Try playing that on the guitar," the soldiers mocked in the stadium in Santiago de Chile, after they tortured his hands. Víctor Jara sang back at them from the ground.

(July, 2003)

40

Praza Do Toural

Early morning.
At the fountain, the junkies
washing their needles.

(30th November)

December

The stall attendant in the hippie market
under the Rúa Nova arches
smells of booze—
stubble beard, and moustache
erratic, skinny man,
pulling the cover
over his stall
as rain hits the plastic.

3 a.m.—I walk home
mist through the Old Town.

Gong! Gong!
Rim of my silence.

Unshaven *gaiteiros* in traditional costume—
black waistcoats, white shirts, black breeches,
flaccid bagpipes over their shoulders,
talking among themselves in the minority language—
like deserters who've walked a long way.
White puttee bandages below their knees,
black knee-breeches—like the battles drummers
from a forgotten peninsular war
falling behind among the prostitutes
and their children, the stumbling camp followers.

Picaresque

Beggars argue, passing women in fur coats.
As a pilgrim limps into the Quintana,
gutter punks, junkies, beggars
lounging on the steps
drinking cartons of wine, perk up.

Loudspeakers on the minarets
of the cathedral
as if for some call to prayer.

January

One stall left in the Rúa Nova.
A woman walks past under an umbrella.
Her cat peeps over an upturned collar.

A small priest, bent over
in his cassock, passes beggars
in the rain. I wonder where to go
in the Quintana dos Mortos,
in the city of time.

Walking out of the city along Rúa do Pombal
in the late afternoon, prostitutes lean in doorways.
They don't call to me, even tiredly. I glimpse
empty beer crates in shebeen bars,
beds behind bead curtains at the back of them.

Glassed-in balconies are sun traps
for women born before the civil war.
White-panelled wood between the panes,
grey-blue double doors, green tendrils
trailing down the grey iron.
Faint wood smoke over the Old Town.

(17th January)

Leaving Thomas' flat into the Rúa do Vilar
and then the cathedral—the Puerta Santa's
closed, won't open for another six years.
Statues of apostles in relief around the door
whisper against each other
behind their hands, as if at shift's end.
Someone's painted their lips with lipstick.

(20th January)

Daily, Quintana

Couples in gold-rimmed sunglasses and English shooting jackets with Collies and Huskies—proud parents of exotics—take over the lower square. Kids on BMXs with training wheels pass me, perched on a rattley orbit. Quarter past five in the afternoon with a hangover *can* be pleasant. Frail perceptions. I'm alive in the sun. Someone's asleep on the bench along the convent wall. Two *Policia Municipal* in blue-black come down the Via Sacra. The beggar who's been shouting, sits down. A hippie woman whistles to her white wolf dog, and goes. The cops stand a while, then stroll on towards the Obradoiro: the public face. A man in a beret swigs from a carton of red wine, scowls at the little girl skipping past in a school uniform and Paddington Bear toggle coat. The punk boy beside him yawns, a knee drawn to his chest. He has a high-shouldered, consumptive look. Tight jeans and red Doc Martens; the West German army surplus coat hangs off him, back cricked from squat living, face like someone coming down.

February

Mist hides the bell tower.
An old lady hobbles down the steps.
Fountains in rain.

A woman in a tight black pencil skirt
—high heels on marble—
passes mahogany confession boxes.
In a side chapel behind glass,
old women in black kneel to the host
in a spiked monstrance silence.
A reclining Templar. By his feet
a black cat. Eve rests
her hand on a skull, time on her hands.

José Antonio Primo de Rivera is inscribed
on the convent wall, beside the huge cross,
over the long stone bench where housewives, students,
junkies sit, south-facing. No one seems to notice the words
being absorbed back into the stone.

(10th February)

Parents drink coffee, their kids in costume.
We're playing pool. Wild music from the street
where a troupe of clowns in red and green
carries a coffin. As if on holiday from cranky,
the old men in the back room burst out singing:
"¡Carnaval! ¡Te quiero!"

(15th February)

Diary

No letters today.
The lottery ticket seller
in the glass booth with venetian blinds
braille-counts a roll of 5,000-pesetas notes.
My lungs' harsh residue.

*

"¡Vamos, hombre!" an old man says
to the rheumatic Alsatian straying behind,
as if to a friend.

*

Four o'clock. Waiters in white jackets and Brilliantine
in *El Paradiso* nod to old women
as they incline, pouring Earl Grey.

*

Two female students link arms
under their umbrella.

A street sweeper in navy overalls,
luminous white stripes at her ankles and sleeves,
a witch's broom sweeping trajectories.

*

The junkies shelter
under the arches in the Toural.
Old men stand beside the police.
The police ignore them, the old men
keep nodding as if they were included.

(21st February)

Plaintive cry of the blind
lottery ticket seller
under the arches of *Correos*
—tickets pinned to his chest—
"¡ONCE para hoy!"

Astringent pines by the Auditorio.
Mist drifting across the houses on the hill
like wood smoke. A smell of damp grass,
or the perennial berries
of suburban fir trees at the end of back gardens
in Dublin. My dead grandfather.

March

Quintana De Vivos

The white wolf dog stalks lozenges of sunlight travelling the convent wall. Two well-dressed ladies go down the steps where I'm sitting: "pues, fíjate María," "mind you, the way these students behave…"—their journey of careful stepping between lounging beggars and self-conscious bohemians takes them out of my hearing.

Reis Católicos

Official cars and local politicians
below Adam and Eve with their fig leaves.
Bodyguards in sunglasses
under angels with genitals.

Long beard-moss on the cathedral.
An agèd foreign couple, white-haired,
strolling. A cherub flying, all cheek.
Eroded lion face watches them out of the stone.

Sea gulls flying in from a storm at sea
—from Iria Flavia,
where the stone boat made landfall.

Two old ladies link arms
in the pre-lunch *paseo*,
one shouting in the other's ear.

A for Anarchism
on baroque stone.

A few tourists already.
British voice.
I grimace, possessive.

April

Alameda

Dove calls of afternoon
I always think are—*cuck-oo*.

*

Two Alsatian pups gambol up, soft-bite
my hands, lick me with heavy tongues,
then run on, play-snarling.

*

A man dozing on a bench
beside a young woman who's writing.
A spider spins between blades of grass.
Breeze, shadows of grass.

*

An old couple stands at the *mirador*
with the famous cathedral view
where wedding pictures are taken.
Brimming bowl.

Evening, Quintana

A fiddler on the steps—
tertulia in Café Literarios.
The open door casts a yellow path
on the flagstones: to warm voices,
points closely-argued,
dark-haired men standing, laughing

—and then 19th century beards,
friends meeting daily at the coffee house
mightn't be that far.

I stop to listen,
then go on.
A man runs past, like a fugitive

the cathedral's towers far above him.
Islamic moon, Jewish star.
Tower of contradictory heart.

Old ladies pant, linking arms
climbing the hill of Costa Vella.
A black cat sits watching
almost in schadenfreude.
In the Obradoiro
the stone is still warm from the sun.

At the five star hotel,
a waiter looks out, closes the door,
making the quiet come closer.

To the west, a spectrum
of blue-black, red-green, darker red,
where the sun is going down.

(11th April)

70

Walking backstreets at lunch:
richness of reused olive oil
from the vents of cheap restaurants.
Someone's eating *tortilla*,
and thin Spanish steaks of *filete*,
ternera, or breaded veal, brown-flecked
from oil's re-frying,
garnished with lemon slice.

A Jack Russell suddenly decides
to bark at two old men
who've been studying the cathedral,
talking, pensive. They jump up the steps
out of the way. One of them bows,
then passes it like a bull fighter.

Workers in their three-wheeler, town council truck
as if inherited from the Eastern Bloc,
holding up the traffic
a mound of cut-grass in the trailer,
laughing, newly-minted bankers
as if rich in what they've cut.

Vai a lavar a cara, pelegrín,
—go wash your face, pilgrim—
it says in red in Galician above a drain
in the Rúa do Val de Deus laneway.

The Punks of the Quintana

You would see them on the steps of the Quintana when Spring had come and it was warm again: a tribe sprawled in the sun amongst the beggars and the gypsies. One day, from the rumble of harsh conversation, a hard laugh reached me. I looked over and saw him: wreathed in dope smoke, standing to stretch himself. His head was shaved except for the fallen yellow Indian crest, and on his chin was a faint stubble. In his boots, earrings and ripped shirt he stood like a tarnished king, wasted arms hanging limp with the suggestion of heroin. I watched him as he moved off—sparse, rangy—breathing him in. His eyes flickering over me as he takes me in: drift into my world.

May

Praza de Entrepraciñas
—"Square Between Small Squares" —
music from an attic.

      *

Rúa do Olvido:
the street of forgetting.

      *

Swans asleep in the rain
pattering on the art deco Moorish pool
in the Alameda—
the name of the park,
it means *grove of poplars*.

Church bells ringing six in the morning.
You can hear the real
rope pull in the ringing.

The young poplars
blow in the breeze
in air that's almost wood smoke.

Faintly—crickets.
White moon in the blue-black sky.
Faint wind saying it's morning.

A cross decipherable in sandstone.
The full moon in a window—in light of which
sometimes I see writing on the stone:
graffiti of an Irish pilgrim. They wrote
El Dinguel de Santiago
in the book of arrivals
then he missed the boat back.

In the empty Quintana, where the hippies
have stubbed their joints out on the steps
and left the roaches, a stream of urine
arrives, running down the Via Sacra
from the doorway of the church
of cloistered nuns
who are at vespers.

The *gitanos* jamming in the Quintana:
the boy on the guitar,
the older man's voice starts up
unsure, shivering—knife.
Two teenaged girls
—eyes of India.
How long since you left home?

The squares quiet
in the north of approaching summer.
The students absent, studying.
The smell of old stone
—the sun starting to dry it—
wet by rain, so many times.

I looked out the window,
Daniela beside me sleeping,
saw a star, looked again,
it was rain on the window.

June

The Book of Beginnings

Women I knew then
who smoked Ducados
would pass me a drag
from time to time
in the Praza de Mazarelos—
black tobacco, the pleasurable
laceration—and me
trying to find the page.

The old woman
wearing her beauty
like dried flowers.
The Iberian confidence
still fresh.

Alameda

Trees hold the breeze.
Sun on the gravel walk
—it diamonds, from mica.

A church bell rings raggedly
in a cloister.
And it's taken up, all over the city.

A couple on the café terrace, laughing.
She takes off her sunglasses;
with one finger, he pushes her lip back
from her teeth. She kisses his finger,
touches his stubble. It hurts.

Old men sit talking
at the Platerías door of the cathedral.
¡Me cago en dios!—"I shit
on God!"—one routinely punctuates.

The arcade arches
of Rúa Nova and Rúa do Vilar
sheltered them in the winter.
Now in late June
they still walk in the shade.

Cicadas make a deeper silence
and summer opens its distances.

Leaving

Owl singing in the quiet night
in the shadow of mingled boughs,
you turn these city trees
into an old wood where I always was.

("The Owl of the Alameda, Lugo", Uxío Novoneyra
Translated by Pearse Hutchinson)

I try to walk away,
stand looking at a fountain
at six in the morning
walking home in the cool June dawn,
the breeze-silence, cut grass in it
or fresh wood smoke:
first fire, or embers of the last.

First Night

After Café Derby, a street led up, up
an incline. Now I know it leads to *Preguntoiro*:
true or not, I translate as the asking place.
I didn't know it was the Old Town, didn't know
anything. In the shops, displays of *tetilla* cheese
and old-fashioned girdles, but—nothing open,
the whole city a brownish stone that glittered.
Out of a narrow alley, the Quintana opened,
and the cathedral reared up. There was no one
—as if the world had retreated, and it was given
to me. Rain dripped from the arches, from everything,
but no rain was falling. I stood there a long time
in the glistening.

Notes

Prohibited under Franco and dismissed as a peasant dialect of Spanish ("español bruto"— "brutish Castilian"—I have heard some say), like Catalan and Basque, *galego* is now recognised by the Spanish government, and is used for official business by the Xunta, the Galician parliament.[5] In accordance with local usage, for the most part this book uses *galego* for street names and place names. However, reflecting the fluidity of daily life, *galego* and Spanish are both used by the people in these poems. In 1993–94, *galego* was typically spoken in the countryside and large towns. Among the cities, Santiago was the exception, especially the city's Old Town, which was the flagship of the language movement. In my Erasmus year, *galego* was spoken by shopkeepers and the fishmongers and butchers of the *Abastos* market—including the older women who walked in from the surrounding countryside to sell their vegetables—as well as by university students, left-wing intellectuals and artists, many of whom were new speakers. In the new town one heard Spanish almost exclusively. Thus, a kind of standoff could ensue between *galego* speakers and those who understood, but persisted in answering in Spanish. (See the poem 'Civil Disagreement'.) The original *Rexurdimento* took place in the 19th century with the poetry of Rosalía de Castro, Eduardo Pondal and Manuel Curros Enríquez, and the recovery of the Cantigas, which were written in Galaico-Portuguese in the 12th-14th centuries.

---

[5] Judgement as to what constitutes a dialect is not separate from the power dynamics that create diglossias. The Diccionario da lingua galega defines diglossia as "Situación dun individuo ou dunha comunidade con dúas linguas de uso, unha delas considerada superior e de prestixo, que é a única empregada nas functions máis elevadas." (Obradoiro / Santillana, Vigo: 1995, p. 317) ("Situation of an individual or a community, with two languages of use, one of which is considered superior and of prestige, which is the only one used in important functions." (My translation.) Far from being a dialect of Castilian, if Galicia were part of Portugal, *galego* would in fact be considered a dialectal variant of Portuguese. I am grateful to my friend Pår Larson of the Opera del Vocabolario Italiano in Florence, an expert in Medieval Italian and an advanced speaker of *galego*, for bringing this to my attention.

***

PAGE 14: The "Old Town" refers to Santiago de Compostela's historic baroque section, known in Spanish as "Ciudad Vieja" or "Casco Antiguo", and in Galician as "Cidade Vella".

PAGE 17: "engominado": gelled. "Tertulia": meeting of friends or associates, literary or otherwise. Ramón del Valle Inclán (1866–1936): Galician-born dramatist.

PAGE 18: "Door of the Sun": La Puerta del Sol is the square at the centre of Madrid from which the distances between Spanish road markers are measured.

PAGE 19: "Colexiata do Sar": The Church of Santa María a Real do Sar.

PAGE 23: "O'Curruncho" ("The Corner", or "Nook"): a bar in the Old Town.

PAGE 25: The "Pórtico da gloria" is a Romanesque portico in Santiago cathedral completed by Master Mateo in 1211. Below it is a piece of marble that has taken on the shape of the hands of the millions of pilgrims who have touched it. Tree of Jesse: typically a depiction of Christ's lineage.

PAGE 26: Tir na nÓg is the "Land of the Young" for which Oisín departs in Irish mythology.

PAGE 27: Al-Andalus generally refers to Moorish or Islamic Iberia. Ducados: a brand of cigarettes of black or dark tobacco. Quilty: a town in West Clare, Ireland.

PAGE 28: "Praza Roxa" (in Galician) was previously (in Spanish, and under Franco), "Plaza José Antonio Primo de Rivera". Primo de Rivera was the founder of the Falange, the nationalist, Fascist party. Executed by the Spanish republican government during the civil war, José Antonio was given cult status under Franco.

PAGE 35: This poem references the statue in Santiago cathedral. The saint as "Moor-slayer" was the mythic product of the Spanish reconquest ("reconquista"), when "Santiago Matamoros" reportedly rode into battle on the Christian Spanish side.

PAGE 37: "Tortilla": Spanish (potato) omelette.

PAGE 38: "Año Santo" / Holy Year takes place when Saint James's Day (25th July) falls on a Sunday. (St. James the Greater is Spain's patron saint.) "Hostal dos Reis Católicos": a five-star luxury hotel in the state-run Parador chain. The "Puerta Santa" / Holy Door of Santiago cathedral in the Quintana square is only open during a Holy Year.

PAGE 40: The "axe and the asp" are symbols of ETA (Euskadi Ta Askatasuna), the Basque separatist group. "Photos of prisoners": common in the Basque Country, less so in Galicia. The "ArmaLite" (or AR-18) is the gun that became synonymous with the IRA. Víctor Jara was the inspirational Chilean singer and Socialist activist who was tortured and murdered on 12th September, 1973, the day after Pinochet's coup, in the stadium in Santiago de Chile subsequently named after him. In republishing an NME piece from 1975, *The Guardian* quotes eye-witness journalist Miguel Cabezas, who was a prisoner in the stadium. Cabezas reported that after the prison camp commandant chopped off Jara's fingers with an axe, Jara staggered up and led 6,000 prisoners in singing the anthem of Unidad Popular, after which the enraged soldiers machine-gunned Jara and the crowd.[6] Other reports are less dramatic, but equally chilling. An article in *National Catholic Reporter* on 22nd June, 2016 states that "Chilean attorney Dennis Navia Perez, who had worked at the university where Jara taught, testified that he was arrested and taken with Jara to the stadium. Once the military recognized Jara, he said, they called him a communist, struck him with rifles and pistols, and broke his hands and wrists so he would "never be able to play the guitar again."[7] Since I use the Jara myth in the poem, it is important here to point out this background in an attempt to delineate the boundaries of what is truth and what is myth.

PAGE 45: "gaiteiro": player of the "gaita", the Galician bagpipes.

PAGE 46: The Quintana is divided into the "Quintana dos Vivos" (of the living) and the "Quintana dos Mortos" (of the dead). The latter was previously a cemetery.

---

[6] Andrew Tyler (2013) 'The life and death of Victor Jara – a classic feature from the vaults', *The Guardian*, 18th September.

[7] Linda Cooper and James Hodge (2016), 'Chilean ex-soldier stands trial for 1973 death of singer Victor Jara', *National Catholic Reporter*, 22nd June.

PAGE 60: "Correos": post office; "ONCE" ("National Organization of Spanish Blind People") often uses its lottery system to raise funds to employ and give benefits to the blind.

PAGE 65: According to local legend, after being martyred by Herod, the remains of St. James were transported via a stone boat, crewed by angels, to Iria Flavia (a bishopric and ancient settlement in what is now Padrón), and then to the site of what would become Santiago de Compostela cathedral: the third-most important site of medieval Christian pilgrimage after Rome and Jerusalem. The first "Xacabeo" (Holy Year) in recent years that was officially promoted by bodies for Galician tourism was in 1993, and was the beginning of state involvement in reviving the Camino de Santiago. The Camino Francés was inscribed on the World Heritage List in 1993.

PAGE 69: "Mirador": viewing point.

PAGE 79: "El Dinguel de Santiago" (the Dingle of Santiago): researchers have discovered evidence of a medieval pilgrimage sea route from Dingle, in western Ireland, to the port city of A Coruña, from which pilgrims would have finished the pilgrimage to Santiago by foot along the Camino Inglés. St. James's church in Dingle was built by Spaniards. Galicians were, doubtless, among them.

PAGE 81: "Gitano": Romani people in Spain famous as the originators of *Flamenco* and *Cante Jondo*. It is said that they originated from Northern India in 600 AD.

PAGE 90: The epigraph is from Pearse Hutchinson's *Done into English: Collected Translations* (The Gallery Press, 2003). Uxío Novoneyra is one of Galicia's most elemental poets. He was from O Courel, the iconic mountain chain in eastern Lugo. The original is:

Moucho que cantas pra noite queda
na sombra das flairas tecidas,
ti fais distas arbres de cidade
un bosque antigo no que eu estuven sempre.

The poem was first published in *Elegías del Caurel y otros poemas* (1966), later republished as *Tempos de elexía* (A Coruña: Vía Láctea, 1991).

© Miles Lowry, www.mileslowry.ca

Born in Dublin in 1972, DAVID MCLOGHLIN is the author of *Waiting for Saint Brendan and Other Poems* (Salmon Poetry, 2012), a section of which was awarded second prize in The Patrick Kavanagh Awards, and *Sign Tongue*, translations from the work of Chilean poet Enrique Winter, which won the 2014 Goodmorning Menagerie Chapbook-in-Translation prize. David received first-class honours from University College, Dublin for his research MA in modern Spanish literature. He also holds an MFA in Poetry from New York University, where he was a Teaching Fellow. David received a major Bursary from The Arts Council / An Chomhairle Ealaíon in 2006, and was the Howard Nemerov Scholar at the 2011 Sewanee Writers' Conference. Between 2003 and 2005 he received three grants to study Galician in Santiago de Compostela. Most recently, he was a prize-winning finalist for the 2015 Ballymaloe International Poetry Prize, judged by Billy Collins. His work has been broadcast on WNYC's Radiolab, and published in journals such as *Poetry Ireland Review, Barrow Street, The Stinging Fly, Cimarron Review, Hayden's Ferry Review* and *Poetry International*. David lives with his wife in Brooklyn, NY.

www.davidmcloghlin.com